The Spiritual World of Ancient China and the Bible

Biblical Background to the Novel
Qin: Dragon Emperor of China

By Brian Godawa

The Spiritual World of Ancient China and the Bible: Biblical Background to the Novel Qin: Dragon Emperor of China
1st Edition

Warrior Poet Publishing
www.warriorpoetpublishing.com

ISBN: 978-1-942858-56-0 (paperback)
ISBN: 978-1-942858-57-7 (ebook)

Scripture quotations taken from *The Holy Bible: English Standard Version.* Wheaton: Standard Bible Society, 2001.

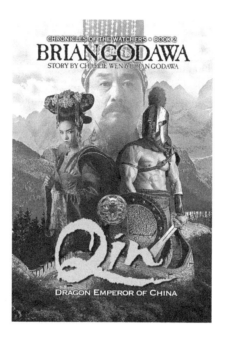

Table of Contents

I receive commissions on all links to Amazon books in this book.

Chapter 1:
The Spiritual World of the Bible

The Gods of the Nations

I explained in the Note to the Reader at the beginning of the novel *Qin: Dragon Emperor of China*, that it is a part of the *Chronicles of the Watchers* series whose books all share what biblical scholar Michael S. Heiser has coined "the Deuteronomy 32 worldview."[1]

I employ this biblical worldview or "divine council" motif as a fantasy element to tell the supernatural side of the story of the first emperor of China. The basic premise is that there is a world of spiritual principalities and powers whose territories are linked to earthly rulers under their authority.

Deuteronomy 32 tells the story of Israel and how she had come to be God's chosen nation. Moses begins by glorifying God and then telling Israel to "remember the days of old"…

> Deuteronomy 32:8–9
> When the Most High gave to the nations their inheritance,
>   when he divided mankind,

---

[1] Michael S. Heiser, *The Unseen Realm: Recovering the Supernatural Worldview of the Bible*, First Edition (Bellingham, WA: Lexham Press, 2015), 113–114.

> he fixed the borders of the peoples
>> according to the number of the sons of God.
> But the Lord's portion is his people,
>> Jacob his allotted heritage.

The context of this passage is the Tower of Babel incident in Genesis 11 when mankind was divided and nations first created. Rebellious humanity sought divinity in unified rebellion, so God separated them by confusing their tongues, which divided them into the seventy nations (of Gentiles) described in Genesis 10. Their ownership of those bordered lands would be the "inheritance" of those peoples.

But inheritance works in heaven as it is on earth. For the people of Jacob (Israel) would become Yahweh's allotted inheritance, and the other seventy Gentile nations were the allotted inheritance of the *Sons of God*.

For more detailed biblical support and explanation, I recommend reading my booklet, *Psalm 82: The Divine Council of the Gods, the Judgment of the Watchers and the Inheritance of the Nations* (paid link). It is the foundation of all three of my novel series, *Chronicles of the Nephilim, Chronicles of the Watchers* and *Chronicles of the Apocalypse*.

So, who were these Sons of God who ruled over the Gentile nations (Psa 82:1-8)? Some believe they were human rulers, others argue for their identities as supernatural principalities and powers. I am in the second camp.

The phrase "Sons of God" is a technical term that means divine beings from God's heavenly throne court (Job 1:6; 38:7) and they are referred to with many different titles. They are sometimes called "heavenly host" (Isa 24:21-22[2]), sometimes called "holy ones" (Deut 33:2-3[3]), sometimes called "the divine council" (Psa 82:1[4]), sometimes called "Watchers" (Daniel 4:13, 17, 23) and sometimes called "gods" or *elohim* in the Hebrew (Deut 32: 17, 43; Psa 82:1; 58:1-2).

Yes, you read that last one correctly. God's Word calls these beings *gods*.

But fear not. That isn't polytheism. The word "god" in this sense is a synonym for "heavenly being" or "divine being" whose realm is that of the spiritual. It does not mean uncreated beings that are all-powerful and all-knowing. Yahweh alone is that God. Yahweh is the God of gods (Deut 10:17; Psa 136:2). He created the other *elohim* ("gods"). These "gods" are created angelic beings who are most precisely referred to as Sons of God.

The narrative is this: before the Flood, some of these heavenly Sons of God rebelled against Yahweh and left their divine dwelling to come to earth (Jude 6), where they violated Yahweh's holy separation and mated with human women (Gen 6:1-4). This was not a racial separation, but a spiritual one. Their corrupt hybrid seed were called "nephilim" (giants), and their effect on humanity included such corruption and violence on the earth that Yahweh sent the Flood to wipe everyone out and start over again with Noah.[5]

---

[2] See also Deut 4:19 with Deut 32:8-9; 1 King 22:19-23.

[3] See also Psa 89:5-7; Heb 2:2.

[4] See also Psa 89:5-7.

[5] For more biblical details on Noah and the Nephilim of Genesis 6, see my book, *When Giants Were Upon the Earth: The Watchers, the Nephilim, and the Biblical Cosmic War of the Seed* (Embedded Pictures Publishing, 2014).

Unfortunately, after the Flood, humanity once again united in evil while building the Tower of Babel, a symbol of idolatrous worship of false gods. So, Yahweh confused their tongues and divided them into the seventy nations. Since man would not stop worshipping false gods, the living God gave them over to their lusts (Rom 1:24, 26, 28) and placed them under the authority of the fallen Sons of God that they worshipped. Fallen spiritual rulers for fallen humanity (Psa 82:1-7). It's as if God said to humanity, "Okay, if you refuse to stop worshipping false gods, then I will give you over to them and see how you like them ruling over you."

Deuteronomy 32 hints at a spiritual reality behind the false gods of the nations, calling them "demons" (Deut 32:17; also Psa 106:37-38). The Apostle Paul later ascribes demonic reality to false gods as well (1 Cor 10:20; 8:4-6). The New Testament continues this ancient notion that spiritual principalities and powers lay behind earthly powers (Eph 6:12; 3:10). The two were inextricably linked in historic events. As Jesus indicated, whatever happened in heaven, also happened on earth (Matt 6:10). Earthly kingdoms in conflict are intimately connected to heavenly powers in conflict.[6]

When earthly rulers battle on earth, the Bible describes the host of heaven battling with them in spiritual unity. In Daniel 10, hostilities between Greece and Persia is accompanied by the battle of heavenly Watchers over those nations (described as spiritual "princes").

---

[6] Dan 10:12-13, 20-21; 2Kgs 6:17; Judges 5:19-20.

Daniel 10:13, 20-21

The prince of the kingdom of Persia withstood me twenty-one days, but Michael, one of the chief princes, came to help me, for I was left there with the kings of Persia." …Then he said, "Do you know why I have come to you? But now I will return to fight against the prince of Persia; and when I go out, behold, the prince of Greece will come. But I will tell you what is inscribed in the book of truth: there is none who contends by my side against these except Michael, your prince.

When Sisera fought with Israel, the earthly kings and heavenly authorities (stars or host of heaven) are described interchangeably in unity.[7]

Judges 5:19–20

"The kings came, they fought; then fought the kings of Canaan…From heaven the stars fought, from their courses they fought against Sisera.

When God punishes earthly rulers, he punishes them along with the heavenly rulers ("host of heaven") above and behind them.

Isaiah 24:21–22

On that day the LORD will punish the host of heaven, in heaven, and the kings of the earth, on the earth. They will be gathered together as prisoners in a pit; they will

---

[7] See also 2 Kings 6:15-17 where Elisha's servant has his spiritual eyes opened to see the myriad of heavenly warriors surrounding Israel preparing to battle Syria.

be shut up in a prison, and after many days they will be punished.[8]

This notion of territorial archons or spiritual rulers is Biblical and carries over into intertestamental literature such as the Book of Enoch and others.[9] It is one of the foundational storylines of this series, Chronicles of the Watchers, as well as Chronicles of the Nephilim and Chronicles of the Apocalypse.

In the Bible, the term "Watchers" only appears in Daniel 4, where a Watcher, also called a "holy one," came down from heaven to proclaim to Daniel the "decree of the Watchers" that Nebuchadnezzar would go mad like a beast (Dan 4:13-17, 23). Though the Watchers of Daniel 4 are not specifically equated with the "princes" over the kingdoms of the nations in Daniel 10, they are considered by ancient Jews to be synonymous. The Watchers over the nations were the princes or principalities of those nations.

Two examples of how the ancient Jews interpreted Deuteronomy 32:8-9 illustrate this notion of territorial principalities watching over nations:

Jubilees 15:31-32
(There are) many nations and many people, and they all belong to him, but over all of them he caused spirits to rule so that they might lead them astray from following

---

[8] Interestingly, this passage of Isaiah is not clear about what judgment in history it is referring to. But the language earlier in the text is similar to the Flood when it says, "For the windows of heaven are opened, and the foundations of the earth tremble. 19 The earth is utterly broken, the earth is split apart, the earth is violently shaken. 20 The earth staggers like a drunken man; it sways like a hut; its transgression lies heavy upon it, and it falls, and will not rise again." So this may be another passage that uses a Flood reference tied in with the Watchers and their punishment.

[9] 1 En. 89:59, 62-63; 67; Jubilees 15:31-32; Targum Jonathan Deut. 32, Sect. LIII; 3Enoch 48C:9, DSS War Scroll 1Q33 Col. xvii:7, Targum Jonathan, Genesis 11, Section II.

him. But over Israel he did not cause any <u>angel or spirit to rule</u> because he alone is their ruler and he will protect them.

Targum Jonathan, Deuteronomy 32, Section LIII
When the Most High made allotment of the world unto the <u>nations</u> which proceeded from the sons of Noach [Noah], in the separation of the writings and languages of the children of men at the time of the division, He cast the lot among the <u>seventy angels, the princes of the nations</u> with whom is the revelation <u>to oversee the city</u>.[10]

But it is the book of 1 Enoch that uses the term "Watchers" most commonly of these territorial princes (or angels or spirits or holy ones). The Sons of God of Genesis 6 are called Watchers all throughout 1 Enoch.[11] And those Sons of God are described in the Old Testament as Yahweh's heavenly host that surround him in his divine council.

Job describes the Sons of God as divine beings who were heavenly host present at the creation (Job 38:4-7), and who gathered around Yahweh, along with the satan, to council with him and perform his decrees (Job 1:6-7; 2:1-6). 1 Kings 22:19-23 depicts these same "host of heaven" as spirits surrounding Yahweh who do his bidding. Psalm

7

82 and 89 describe the assembly of heavenly host as his "divine council" of "gods," "holy ones," and "Sons of the Most High" (82:6).

All these terms are used synonymously for the divine beings of God's heavenly host, the Sons of God to whom Deuteronomy 32:8 declared were allotted the nations for an inheritance to watch over (territorial powers).

So the Bible says that there is demonic reality to false gods. But since those Sons of God who were territorial authorities over the nations were spiritually fallen Watchers, that makes them demonic or evil in essence. So what if they are the actual demonic beings behind the false gods of the ancient world? What if the fallen Sons of God were masquerading as the gods of the nations in order to keep humanity enslaved in idolatry to their authority? That would affirm the Biblical stories of earthly events with heavenly events occurring in synchronization.

That is the biblical premise of the *Chronicles of the Watchers*. The pagan gods, like Yu Huang and the Three Pure Ones in the novel *Qin*, are actually fallen Sons of God, Watchers of the nations, crafting false identities and narratives as gods of the nations that are connected and reflected in the earthly events of human history and its rulers. For a detailed biblical defense of this interpretation see my booklet, *Psalm 82: The Divine Council of the Gods, the Judgment of the Watchers and the Inheritance of the Nations.* (paid link)

Leviathan

Leviathan is a crucial character in the Chronicles universe. He shows up in Chronicles of the Nephilim, Chronicles of the Apocalypse, as well as Chronicles of the Watchers. He is drawn from the ancient Near Eastern worldview that permeates the Bible.

Contrary to what some hyper-literalists may think, Leviathan is not a real world sea dinosaur or even an extinct sea monster, it is a spiritual image that was used by ancient Near Eastern religions to symbolize the chaos of the cosmos that their god fought to bring about his rule and order. The Babylonians called it Tiamat, the Canaanites called it Lotan, the Ugaritic translation for "Leviathan." Hebrews called it Leviathan and sometimes Rahab.[12]

The battle of divinity to create order out of chaos is called "chaoskampf" by theologians.[13] In Mesopotamian religion, Marduk defeated Tiamat the sea dragon and split her in half to create the heavens and earth that symbolized the establishment of Babylonian world power.[14] The Canaanite Baal defeated the Sea (Yam), River (Nahar) and Leviathan (Lotan) in order to become the Most High ruler of the Canaanite pantheon.[15]

---

[12] Leviathan: Job 3:8; 41; Psa 74:13-14; Psa 104:26; Isa 27:1. Leviathan is said to dwell in the Abyss in Job 41:24 (LXX). "[Leviathan] regards the netherworld [Tartauros] of the deep [Abyss] like a prisoner. He regards the deep [Abyss] as a walk." Job 41:34, Tan, Randall, David A. deSilva, and Logos Bible Software. The Lexham Greek-English Interlinear Septuagint. Logos Bible Software, 2009.

For Rahab, see: Isa 51:9; Job 9:13; 26:12-13; Ps 87:4; Psalm 89:9-10.

[13] For Chaoskampf in the Bible, see: Psalm 89:9-10; Isaiah 51:9-10; Job 26:12-13. Psalms 18, 29, 24, 29, 65, 74, 77, 89, 93, and 104. Also, Exodus 15, Job 9, 26, 38, and Isaiah 51:14-16; 2 Samuel 22.

[14] *Enuma Elish*, Tablet IV, lines 104-105, 137-138, 144.

[15] See KTU 1.3:3.38-41.

So, Yahweh is depicted as defeating Leviathan to establish his covenantal order with Israel at Sinai.

> Psalm 74:13–17
> You divided the sea by your might;
> > you broke the heads of the sea monsters on the waters.
> You crushed the heads of Leviathan;
> > you gave him as food for the creatures of the wilderness.
> You split open springs and brooks;
> > you dried up ever-flowing streams.
> Yours is the day, yours also the night;
> > you have established the heavenly lights and the sun.
> You have fixed all the boundaries of the earth;
> > you have made summer and winter.

In the Psalm above, the Red Sea deliverance of the Israelites ("dividing the sea") was the metaphor of God taking them out of the chaos of pagan Egypt. As in other ancient religions, Yahweh is depicted as defeating the sea, which also represented chaos to land dwellers. And Leviathan is in that sea as its instrument of power. But Yahweh crushes the heads of the sea dragon of chaos, and the creatures of the desert feast on his body. This banquet of eating the flesh of Leviathan symbolizes Yahweh's victory and is a common theme that appears in both biblical and extrabiblical Jewish poetry.[16]

The book of Revelation describes the victory of Christ over his enemies in chapter 19 as the "great supper of God" where the birds of prey eat the flesh of his defeated foes (19:17). While Leviathan is not

---

[16] For 2nd Temple examples of the feast of Leviathan and Behemoth, see 4Ezra 6:47-52; 2Apoc. Bar. 29:4; 1 Enoch 60: 7-9, 24.

included in this Revelation passage, it is the same kind of nature banquet motif as described in Psalm 74: creatures feasting on the flesh of the enemies of God. The "banquet of flesh" was a common way of symbolizing deliverance from and victory over one's enemies.

And Leviathan does show up in Revelation as the seven-headed sea dragon who is the satanic enemy of chaos against God's people.[17] Once again, the sea dragon's defeat is symbolically linked to God establishing a new order, namely the new covenant kingdom of God in Christ's blood (Rev 12:9-11).

But did the monster grow some new heads in Psalm 74? Not necessarily. If one looks closely at the fourteenth verse, even in the Hebrew, it says that Leviathan has multiple *heads*, plural, not *head*, singular (Yahweh "crushed the *heads* of Leviathan"). And it is no coincidence that the Leviathan of the Canaanite Baal epic has seven heads.[18]

But the last component of Psalm 74 above is the creation language that reminds the reader of Genesis 1. Yahweh separates day and night, establishes the heavenly host and makes the seasons (v. 15-17). This is not some unconnected jump back to the creation of the universe, it is another cosmic metaphor of the covenant in terms of a "heaven and earth." Right after Yahweh delivers them through the sea, he brings them to Sinai, where he establishes his covenant order. The Mosaic covenant was a spiritual cosmos, a heaven and earth of God's operations with his people. Yahweh delivers his people, destroys the dragon of

---

[17] See Rev 12:3-13:4; 16:13-16; 20:2-3.
[18] KTU 1.5:1:30

11

chaos with victory and creates his covenantal order with Israel, a new "cosmos."

Hyper-literalist assumptions may cause distress in the believer who thinks this would mean that the Red Sea deliverance was "just a myth" or a spiritual symbol that didn't really happen in history. But this is simply a misunderstanding of the nature of ancient storytelling. Everything is not all "literal" or all "symbolic." It is very common for biblical writers to describe historic events with poetic or symbolic flair. So the Red Sea deliverance connected to the Sinai covenant was an historic event, but it had spiritual ramifications that were so important they had to be described using symbolic terms of Leviathan and creation.

Leviathan cannot be a literal physical creature, because it is destroyed and eaten here in Psalm 74, yet it is described by Isaiah as being alive again then slain *in the future* at another victory of God, namely, the coming of Messiah (Isa 27:6, 9). Leviathan is a spiritual symbol of the chaos that battles against order through history.

> Isaiah 27:1
> In that day the LORD with his hard and great and strong
> sword will punish Leviathan the fleeing serpent,
> Leviathan the twisting serpent, and he will slay the
> dragon that is in the sea.

But this *chaoskampf* in the Bible is not the same as pagan versions of it, where there is a dualist equivalence between the combatants, and either one might win. For example, Genesis 1 depicts Leviathan very differently for its theological purpose. We read of God's Spirit hovering over the dark "face of the deep" (v. 2), which is "without form and void," or "an unfilled wasteland" (Hebrew: *tohu wa-bohu*), an expression of that chaos that the sea tends to represent to the ancient world. The Hebrew word behind "deep" is *tehom*, which scholars argue is a linguistic connection to that sea dragon Tiamat. But in this context, there is no *chaoskampf* battle depicted. God simply speaks and order is established through the separation of things.

And then when a dragon appears, it is simply one of many sea creatures that God created to swarm in the sea.

> Genesis 1:21
> So God created the great sea creatures [*tannim*] and every living creature that moves, with which the waters swarm... And God saw that it was good.

The Hebrew word for "sea creatures" (*tannim*) is a word that is translated elsewhere as *dragon*.[19] Though Leviathan is not used here, the intent of the chapter is to demythologize the elements of the natural world that pagan cultures had divinized, including not only the sun, moon and stars, but the sea (chaos) and the dragons that resided there.

So, the imagery of *chaoskampf*, sea and dragon, are used poetically in some Bible passages to communicate the notion of God's creation of order out of chaos, but in other passages, those mythopoeic symbols are tamed with ease and without a dualistic struggle because they are after all symbols in the service of their creator.[20] Leviathan has no chance of

---

[19] Isaiah 51:9. "Serpent, dragon, sea-monster" Francis Brown, Samuel Rolles Driver, and Charles Augustus Briggs, *Enhanced Brown-Driver-Briggs Hebrew and English Lexicon* (Oxford: Clarendon Press, 1977), 1072.

[20] In Job 41, God's questions to Job about being able to make Leviathan a servant or "play with him as with a bird" are obvious implications that God does so with Leviathan as a domesticated pet. See also Psalm 104:26. See also "sea creatures" (tannim: dragons) Psalm 148:7; Psalm 74:13; Isa 51:9.

winning in the Bible as he does in pagan mythology. All things are subject to the sovereign control of Yahweh, even chaos and evil.

See my book, *When Giants Were Upon the Earth* (paid link) for more on the theological meaning of Leviathan and its interaction with other fantastical motifs in the Bible.

Chapter 2:
The Characters

The Story First

Many of my readers like to learn about the biblical and historical research behind my novels after they have read them. The fact behind the fiction. It helps bring context and explains some of the "stranger things" of the novels to those who are intellectually and spiritually curious. This booklet is a presentation of the research behind my novel, *Qin: Dragon Emperor of China*. But the truth is that the material in this book is so fascinating that it can be read on its own by those who hunger as I do to uncover the biblical background to history.

The novel begins in 220 B.C. in the Babylonian region of the Seleucid empire. The Greek kingdom of Antiochus the Great is crumbling with the winds of revolt. And in the midst of it all, mysterious mercenaries from the Far East slip into Babylon and kidnap a magus from the temple. Magi are the masters of both magic and science, but Antiochus doesn't know why they were chosen as hostages.

So the king sends his bastard son and disgraced warrior Antiochus the Younger into the mysterious land of the Far East with two goals: find the magus and capture a mythical creature that will give the Greek king absolute power: a dragon.

Antiochus the Younger travels to that distant land, ruled by its first emperor, Qin Shi Huang di ("Cheen Shir Hwong Dee"). The Greek warrior discovers a world of both wonder and danger. A contrast and comparison of cultures. A clash of civilizations. Antiochus falls in love with one of the emperor's concubines and he discovers the spiritual truth behind the mythological dragon that protects that world.

What's worse, the emperor is seeking the elixir of immortality. He has forced his own alchemists and scientists to find it before the emperor dies so he can obtain eternal life and rule forever. And he will sacrifice anything and anyone to achieve his goal.

As Antiochus negotiates the treacherous politics of his presence in the land of Qin (spelled in the novel as "Ch'in" from where we get "China"), he also discovers there is a spiritual past to China that the emperor has suppressed. And that past goes back to the infamous Tower of Babel in Genesis 11, where God confused the tongues of the nations in order to stop mankind from the pursuit of divinity. The concubine has spiritual ties to that heritage and the emperor wants her eliminated.

Antiochus and the concubine find themselves on the run to the Great Wall of China where a revolt of slaves breaks out just as barbarians are at the gates of the wall, trying to break in. Unfortunately, the dragon is empowering the emperor's armed forces and Antiochus and the concubine have only one chance to defeat the darkness. They must fight their way to the ancient Altar of Heaven to rekindle the lost power of Shang Di, the true creator God of China's past.

A unique aspect of the novel is the depiction of the spiritual world. The novel pulls back the curtain of the unseen realm. It depicts the "spiritual principalities and powers" that reign behind pagan Gentile nations and how they have influence on the course of history. The gods of ancient China are not mere myths without bite. They are actually demonic powers that are real and have their own agenda.

Thus the god Yu Huang, the supreme head of the Chinese pantheon of gods, seeks to maintain his power over the emperor and his land much like human mobsters might maneuver for power over their regions in a city under their control.

Though this is obviously fantastic and speculative, the principle of spiritual warfare is biblical. There were spiritual entities of power ruling over Gentile nations as depicted in Deuteronomy 32:8-10 and Psalm 82 (explained in chapter 1). The storyline of these spiritual powers is intended to reflect the mythology of pagans and how it reflects spiritual reality within a biblical worldview.

And that is the basic storyline of the novel *Qin: Dragon Emperor of China*. Historical fantasy based on spiritual fact. Now, enjoy learning about the historical and biblical research behind it all…

Xeneotas (Antiochus the Younger)

The protagonist of the novel is a Greek warrior general, Xeneotas, the secret bastard son of Antiochus III of Seleucia, known as Antiochus the Great. Xeneotas is a fictional character based very loosely on a real general of Seleucia of similar name. His family status is creative license.

Historically, General Xeneotas fought against the rebel Molon who launched his forces against the capital city named Seleucia on the Tigris

River in 221 B.C. Xeneotas foolishly pursued Molon into an ambush and was killed in that battle, which resulted in the temporary loss of Babylonia for King Antiochus. It would take a year for the king to defeat Molon and quell the rebellion.[1]

In the novel, I make Xeneotas fail that battle in Babylon by the same trick of Molon, but instead of dying, Xeneotas survives and is sent off into the Far East on a secret journey from which he will not return. So his presumed death fits the "space between" the facts, fictional though it may be.

And Xeneotas' fictional bastard status in the novel is not without historical precedent. Most kings, including Antiochus III had concubines and other wives. So making Xeneotas the first-born son of a beloved concubine would justify him claiming the name of Antiochus the Younger, should he win his father's approval. Historically, there were many Antiochuses in the family line. Making The Younger's personal journey one that was lost to history along with his identity, again makes it at least conceivable if not actually historical.

Xeneotas' father Antiochus the Great as well as his military general Hermias, and their political struggles are based on true events.

The Magi

The Babylonian magi in the novel are also fictional characters, but drawn from the historical tradition of the prophet Daniel's influence on

---

[1] Michael Taylor. *Antiochus the Great.* Pen and Sword. Kindle Edition. Location 654 of 4228.

Babylonia four hundred years earlier. "According to Herodotus, [magi] were members of a Persian priestly caste who specialized in astrology, interpretation of dreams, and magic."[2]

During the time of the Babylonian captivity of Judah, the young Hebrew prisoner Daniel had been able to accurately interpret the troubling dreams of King Nebuchadnezzar when the "wise men" of the royal court could not. Those wise men included "magicians, enchanters, sorcerers and Chaldeans" (Dan 2:2, 10). The Greek word used to translate "magician" in the Septuagint (LXX) was "magi."

Daniel had made such an impression upon the king that he placed the Hebrew lad in power over those wise men, as well as over all of Babylon.

> Daniel 2:47–48
> The king answered and said to Daniel, "Truly, your
> God is God of gods and Lord of kings, and a revealer
> of mysteries, for you have been able to reveal this
> mystery." Then the king gave Daniel high honors and
> many great gifts, and made him ruler over the whole
> province of Babylon and chief prefect over all the wise
> men of Babylon.

Daniel went on to also impress Nebuchadnezzar's successors, King Belshazzar, and Darius the Mede. In short, the humble Hebrew prophet had achieved so much influence over his pagan captors' own magicians, enchanters, sorcerers and Chaldeans, that by the first century of the Roman Empire, Babylonian wise men ("magi") from the East had come

---

[2] W. W. Buehler, "Wise Men (NT)," ed. Geoffrey W. Bromiley, *The International Standard Bible Encyclopedia, Revised* (Wm. B. Eerdmans, 1979–1988), 1084.

searching for the Messiah based on their astrological teachings. They clearly got that information from Daniel.

This is not to say that the Babylonian system was fully Yahwist or that the magi of the Nativity story of Jesus were Jewish converts. But at least we can say that Daniel's teaching of the coming Messiah lasted for 600 years within the Babylonian magi tradition.

And therein lies the connection with the magi of the novel *Qin: Dragon Emperor of China*. They too are looking for that Danielic Messiah, an apparent reflection of the Chinese search for the one who would unify all under heaven.

The dominant text of the Babylonian magi that shows up in the novel is the *Enuma Anu Enlil*, an astrological text for interpreting the omens of celestial movements. The astrology of the ancient Near East is not the same as today. Though the Babylonians did develop their understanding of the Zodiac as influencing life on earth, it was not so simple as the modern horoscope in the newspaper. It was a commonplace tradition in the ancient Near East that the stars were gods, and that the divine embraced the whole of what we would now call "nature."[3] Therefore the effect of the heavens upon earthly destinies could be divined through understanding celestial mechanics. But it was first understood that astrology related to collective entities, political powers, nations and royalty. Only after 500 B.C. did it begin to be applied to individual lives of the lesser classes.[4]

---

[3] Francesca Rochberg, *In the Path of the Moon: Babylonian Celestial Divination and Its Legacy* (Netherlands: Koninklijke Brill NV, 2010), 22.

[4] Rochberg, *In the Path of the Moon*, 189.

The names of the magi in the novel are Balthazar, Melchior and Gaspar. The astute reader will recognize those names as the names of the three magi (or "wise men") in church tradition who visited the child Jesus in Bethlehem. Though the biblical text does not say there were three magi nor does it give their names, western tradition has suggested there were three because of the three gifts brought: gold, frankincense and myrrh (Matthew 2:11).

An even more astute reader will notice that those magi are 600 years before Christ, rendering them impossible candidates for a visit to young Jesus. Hopefully, the reader has already read the novel for the explanation of that historical anomaly. If you haven't, I won't ruin it for you by revealing the answer here.

Ch'in Shih Huang Di

The emperor's name is pronounced in English as "Cheen Shure Hwong Dee." This character in the novel *Qin: Dragon Emperor of China* was based upon the historical first emperor of China, the first to unify seven warring kingdoms under one ruler. The spelling used in the novel is from the older Wade-Giles translation of Chinese (Ch'in Shih Huang Di). I did this because it would be easier to read in English, and because it also hints at the origin of the name for China as the land of Ch'in (Qin). The more common spelling today would be Qin Shi Huang Di.

Before the Qin empire, the land which we now call "China" was divided into seven kingdoms and was named by her inhabitants *Tianxia*, meaning "under heaven."[5] Like most ancient civilizations, the Chinese considered their land to be the center of the earth, or as they put it, *Zhong Guo*, the "Central Nation." We now translate that as "Middle Kingdom."[6]

The actual inspiration for empire came from the previous four hundred years of Chinese internicine warfare of kingdoms called The Warring States period. Seven major states (kingdoms) fought for dominance of the region until the Qin state achieved final conquest and united the seven kingdoms under one ruler, the emperor. That emperor was Qin Shi Huang Di.

The emperor's historical origins have a rumor of suspicion behind them that is hinted at in the novel. Before he became emperor, his name was Ying Zheng. He was ostensibly the son of Yiren, the king of Qin. The queen, Ying Zheng's mother, was also the secret lover of a merchant advisor to the king named Lu Buwei. There is significant historical evidence that points to Ying Zheng as the illegitimate son of the queen and Lu Buwei.[7]

When Zheng became the first (*shi*) emperor, he used his family name Qin and added the old Eastern term for supreme rulers, *Huang Di*. Thus he became Qin shi Huang Di, the first supreme ruler of the house of Qin ruling over all under heaven. But adding that "Di," would prove to be a deliberate claim to divinity.

---

[5] Denis Twitchett and John K. Fairbank, eds., *The Cambridge History of China: Volume 1: The China and Han Empires, 221 B.C. — A.D. 220* (Cambridge University Press, 1999), 20.

[6] Dr. Thong, *Faith Of Our Fathers*, Kindle edition, Location 236 of 344.

[7] Jonathan Clements, *The First Emperor of China* (Albert Bridge Books, 2006, 2015), 45.

The will of God (Di) in the choice of government was called "The Mandate of Heaven" because the word "heaven" was often used as a stand-in for God himself. The Mandate would be similar to what the West called "the divine right of kings." The emperor's authority was derived from God, so the emperor was called "Son of Heaven." If the emperor did not fulfill the divine mandate, he would be punished by heaven.[8]

But China scholar John Man explains that the word "Di" in the emperor's name was a term of highest supernatural power. "Huang Di, often translated as August Emperor, thus declaring himself imperial ruler, god, sage and ancestor all in one."[9] Like all tyrants of the world, the first Chinese emperor set a standard of divinity in the office that would continue for centuries.

Huang Di would become known for his peculiar pursuit of eternal life to maintain that divine status. He had ordered his magicians and scholars to create the elixir of immortality through alchemy, and he had sent explorers to find the mythical Isle of Immortals to bring back the elixir should they find it.

It was believed at the time by Daoists that certain metals and elements like gold, mercury ("quicksilver"), arsenic and others, if ingested in small amounts would lengthen life.[10] So, while waiting for his magicians to achieve their alchemic ambitions, the emperor had a regular diet of mercury and arsenic baked into small cakes for easy

---

[8] Dr. Thong, *Faith Of Our Fathers*, Kindle edition, Location 240 and 244 of 344.

[9] John Man, *The Terra Cotta Army: China's First Emperor and the Birth of a Nation* (Cambridge, MA: Da Capo Press, 2008), 74.

[10] Man, *Terra Cotta Army*, 102.

consumption. As described in the novel, one of the procedures of creating the elixir attempted by the Chinese "supernatural scholars" was that of turning a red crystal, cinnabar, into mercury. Metal poisoning is now widely considered to be the cause of the emperor's perpetual sickness and ultimate insanity.

In the novel, Huang Di's descent into bad health and madness was drawn from a sixth century's record of observations of the effects of such metal poisoning, where the very ill effects themselves were ironically considered "evidence" of the purging of sickness:

> After taking an elixir, if your face and body itch as
> though insects were crawling over them, if your hands
> and feet swell dropsically, if you cannot stand the smell
> of food and bring it up after you have eaten it, if you
> feel as though you were going to be sick most of the
> time, if you experience weakness in your four limbs, if
> you have to go often to the latrine, or if your head or
> stomach violently ache – do not be alarmed or
> disturbed. All these effects are merely proofs that the
> elixir you are taking is successfully dispelling your
> latent disorders.[11]

Huang Di's pursuit of immortality also included a search for the mythical Isle of Immortals. In the novel he sends a Chinese "wise man" Xu Fu to find the magical Isle based on the explorer's reports. This is based on historical fact. Xu Fu had told Huang Di about the Isle and about three spirit mountains where the immortals lived: Penglai, Fangzhang, and Yingzhou. But when pressed to find it, Xu Fu claimed

---

[11] Man, *Terra Cotta Army*, 102.

that it was impossible for normal men to go there. Only wizards, or pure boys or maidens could approach it. He was then allowed to bring with him 1000 virgin boys and girls to find the Isle and bring back the elixir of immortality.[12] God only knows what Xu Fu really did to those innocent youth.

As in the novel, so in real life, Xu Fu returned and made an excuse for his inability to get to the Isle: It was guarded by large sea monsters. So the emperor took his counselor, Li Ssu and his youngest son, Huhai, and went off to kill the Great Fish with a large crossbow. By now, the emperor's madness had taken him over on his impossible quest. He shot some fish in the sea and died on the road back to his palace.[13]

The novel covers this incident but adds a fantasy element of fighting the sea dragon Leviathan. The story retains the historical facts out of it: Huang Di dies on that trip, and Li Ssu and Huhai return with the intent to take the throne for Huhai. The fantasy genre becomes a way to picture the spiritual reality of what is going on in the earthly realm.

In fact, this was a common goal of mine as I wrote the story. All the fantasy elements were added in a way that would not contradict what happened historically, but rather support the facts with mythopoeic spirituality.

---

[12] Sima Qian, (2011-02-10). *Records of the Grand Historian: Qin Dynasty* (p. 49). Columbia University Press. Kindle Edition.

[13] Clements, *The First Emperor*, 156.

Brian Godawa

Miscellaneous Factoids

Many of the activities of the emperor described in the novel *Qin: Dragon Emperor of China* are rooted in historical facts. He is depicted as unifying all of China in terms of government, measurement systems, money and travel. He is responsible for completing the "Great Wall" of China, referred to as the "Long Wall" or "Long Cemetery" by his people. He did entomb the bodies of laborers into the Wall as the novel indicated.[14] He also burned all the books of previous history and philosophy, such as the Chinese *Classics*. He wanted to erase the traditional wisdom of Confucius and others and replace it with Legalism, a new Machiavellian political philosophy that rejected tradition and family legacy for power. He also murdered 450 of his "scholars" because of their disagreement with this revolutionary policy.[15]

One curious artifact of history that makes it into the novel is the existence of gigantic warrior statues cast by the emperor as spiritual guardians of his realm. Ancient Chinese historian Sima Qin writes, "According to some reports, these colossal figures, which each weighed the equivalent of nearly twenty-nine English tons, represented twelve giants wearing "barbarian" garb who appeared at Lintao in Gansu... The

---

[14] Clements, *The First Emperor of China* (Kindle Locations 1903-1907). Kindle Edition.

[15] Dr. Thong, *Faith Of Our Fathers*, Kindle edition, Location 292-293 of 344.

On the burning of scholars: Sima Qian, *Records of the Grand Historian: Qin Dynasty*, (Columbia University Press, 2011), Kindle Edition, 55.

statues were said to have survived until the close of the Eastern Han."[16] Is this evidence of Nephilim? Not for historical purposes, but for fantasy fictional purposes, yes indeed. Though recent archeological discoveries do indicate that giants are not entirely absent from ancient Chinese history.[17]

As a side note, though the characters and political issues of generals Meng Tian, Fan Zhao, scholar Xu Fu, counselor Li Ssu, and the imperial sons Huhai and Fusu are based on historical facts, the characters of the concubine Mei Li and the warrior Wu Shu are fictional.

---

[16] Sima Qian, *Records of the Grand Historian: Qin Dynasty,* (Columbia University Press, 2011), Kindle Edition, footnote 77, page 245.

[17] For giants discovery see: https://www.smithsonianmag.com/smart-news/graveyard-giants-found-china-180963976/

Chapter 3:
The Spiritual World of China

Tower of Babel and the Tomb of Qin

In the novel *Qin: Dragon Emperor of China*, reference is made to Chinese oracle bones that record contact between King Cyrus of Persia and the Chinese in the sixth century B.C., four hundred years before the Qin dynasty. This is based on real modern discoveries of cuneiform clay cylinders about Cyrus the Great and his conquest of Babylon that match those found on Chinese oracle bones in China.[1] The ancient Babylonians most likely had interaction with the ancient Chinese.

But there is also biblical evidence of that connection. As explained in Chapter 1, the Tower of Babel incident in Genesis 11 is a foundational narrative to the Deuteronomy 32 worldview, or as I call it, "the Watcher paradigm" that guides the Chronicles of the Watchers series along with its sister series, Chronicles of the Nephilim and Chronicles of the Apocalypse.

This paradigm understands the fallen biblical Watchers over the nations to be identical or connected to the gods of the Gentile nations.

---

[1] See http://zoroastrianheritage.blogspot.com/2013/03/cyrus-edict-chinese-cuneiform-bones.html

And these gods were allotted the various nations as their "inheritance" of ownership. Every Gentile nation territory was under the authority of the demonic false gods that they worshipped.

By way of review, the Tower of Babel was a ziggurat step pyramid that was built as a "stairway to heaven" for the gods to come down and meet with priests in the temple at the top of the pyramid. The word for Babylon in Akkadian is *babil-ani*, which means "gate of the gods."[2] This temple tower symbolized a "cosmic mountain," and its basic pyramidal structure is apparent in most ancient civilizations across the globe, from Mesopotamia to Egypt to India to South America.[3]

One theory that explains this uniformity of structure across geographically and culturally diverse civilizations is that the original unified people at Babel were split up by God at the Confusion of Tongues incident and brought with them their knowledge of such sacred architecture. The biblical word "Babel" is a polemical mockery of the Akkadian name of Babylon that turns the "gate of gods" into "confusion."

One of those separated seventy nations from Babel would end up settling in the territory we now call China. Modern Chinese researcher Dr. Thong, Chan Kei writes,

> I have now come to the studied conclusion that the
> ancient Chinese were one of the many original nations
> dispersed after the confusion of languages at the Tower
> of Babel, described in Genesis 11 of the Bible. Some

---

[2] Anne Habermehl, "Where in the World Is the Tower of Babel?", *Answers Research Journal 4* (2011):30. www.answersingenesis.org/contents/379/arj/v4/Tower_Babel.pdf

[3] See: https://www.touropia.com/step-pyramids-of-the-world/

among these dispersed nations were alienated from God, while others wanted to follow His way. Like the Pilgrims who went to America to preserve the purity of their religious beliefs, the people group that went on to found the Chinese civilization was, I believe, a God-fearing race that desired to worship God appropriately.[4]

Another researcher of this issue, C.H. Kang concludes the same Babel origin of China at the Great Dispersion, concluding that because of China's geographical isolation, it was cut off from the outside influence of the west and thus remained relatively undisturbed for 2000 years. This isolation meant that it retained a stronger connection to its Babel origins (and therefore Yahweh) than did the other nations.[5]

I bring up this information about ziggurats because the tomb of the Chinese emperor Qin Shi Huang Di is in the shape of a ziggurat. Though it currently resides beneath an unexcavated dirt mound called Mount Li located in the Shaanxi province of China, artistic renderings of the tomb indicate its pyramid shape.[6]

Though the tomb has never been opened, descriptions of the interior by Chinese historians and the like conjure rivers of mercury and a sky ceiling of gems as stars over the floor created as a map of the world.[7] The novel *Qin* depicts these historical elements as well as the famous army of thousands of terra cotta soldiers created as guardians in

---

[4] Dr. Thong, Chan Kei, *Faith Of Our Fathers: Finding God In Ancient China* (Singapore: Cru Asia Limited, 2018), Kindle edition, Location 24 of 344.

[5] C.H. Kang, *The Discovery of Genesis: how the Truths of Genesis Were Found Hidden in the Chinese Language* (St. Louis, MO: Concordia House, 1979), 2-3.

[6] See the artistic rendering of the tomb: https://www.uchinavisa.com/qin-shi-huang.html

[7] Sima Qian, *Records of the Grand Historian: Qin Dynasty*, (Columbia University Press, 2011), Kindle Edition, footnote 77, page 64.

the afterlife.[8] It was also a fact that the emperor's concubines as well as the designers of the tomb were sealed in alive in the structure after the emperor was buried in it.[9]

So, who were the gods this temple tower mausoleum of Qin was servicing? Let's find out.

The Dragon

The dragon is a well-known symbol of ancient Chinese history and mythology. Whereas the western tradition of dragons is of a fire breathing dinosaur-like behemoth, the Chinese dragon is born of water and is long and snake-like with small legs. These opposing images reflect a much deeper difference of spiritual understanding.

As classicist scholar M.W. de Visser explains, the dragon appears in the oldest of Chinese literature, the *I Ching,* a divination text that dates back to the second millennium B.C. The dragon is a positive image of power.

> [It] symbolizes those among men who are fullest of
> Light, namely great men, and its appearance is
> considered to be an omen of their coming, i.e. of their
> birth. In the first place the greatest and fullest of Yang
> among them all, the Emperor, is, of course, symbolized

---

[8] Clara Moskowitz, "The Secret Tomb of China's 1st Emperor: Will We Ever See Inside?"
https://www.livescience.com/22454-ancient-chinese-tomb-terracotta-warriors.html

[9] Jonathan Clements, *The First Emperor of China* (Kindle Locations 2901-2903). Kindle Edition.

by the dragon. He is, indeed, the representative of Imperial power.[10]

From the Zhou dynasty onward (1122-249 B.C.) the dragon was used exclusively of rulers.[11] Visser reveals that the emperor Qin Shi Huang Di applied it specifically to himself, and even described him employing winged dragons in his battle with rebels, much like the fantasy battle at the Great Wall in the *Qin* novel.

Qin Shi Huang Di was referred to as the "Ancestral Dragon" in the ancient Chinese *Historical Records* by Sima Qian.[12] Qin was one of the first emperors to set himself up as a personification of the dragon, and he is considered the first to introduce dragon worship into the Chinese culture.[13]

In ancient Chinese literature, the dragon is a heavenly creature that symbolizes personal power, the origin of earthly creatures and wisdom.[14] The Chinese *Classics* compiled by Confucius describe the dragon as a god of thunder, clouds and rain, essentially a storm god.[15]

In the Bible, the dragon is clearly understood to be a negative image. As explained in the section on Leviathan, the sea dragon is a symbol of chaos that battles against the Creator's natural and covenantal

---

[10] Marinus Willem de Visser, *The Dragon in China and Japan* (Ithica, NY; Cornell University Library, 1913), 38.

[11] Dr. Thong, *Faith Of Our Fathers*, Kindle edition, Location 200 of 344.

[12] Dr. Thong, *Faith Of Our Fathers*, Kindle edition, Location 280 of 344.
Visser, *The Dragon in China*, 122.

[13] Dr. Thong, *Faith Of Our Fathers*, Kindle edition, Location 290 of 344.

[14] Visser, *The Dragon in China*, 62-65.

[15] Visser, *The Dragon in China*, 109-115.

order (Psalm 74). The Serpent of the Garden is cursed for his deception and lies (Genesis 3:14). His "seed" or offspring are prophesied to be at war with the messianic "seed of Eve," biting the heel that crushes his head (Genesis 3:15). This poetic prediction of the coming Messiah runs through the entire Bible as a picture of Satan's people trying to destroy God's people. And that serpent becomes linked to Satan as the seven-headed sea dragon of chaos in the final dissolution of the Old Covenant, a dragon who also seeks to kill Christians (Revelation 12:4-6).

> Revelation 12:9
> And the great dragon was thrown down, that ancient serpent, who is called the devil and Satan, the deceiver of the whole world…

This contrast of interpretation comes to play in the novel as the biblical reality of the satanic Watchers is unveiled behind the earthly Chinese dragons.

One other tangent related to dragons in the story of *Qin: Dragon Emperor of China* was the red herring thrown out by the emperor to discourage the protagonist's pursuit of a dragon. Huang Di shows Antiochus a graveyard of "dragon bones" to argue that dragons are long dead and therefore only a legend in the present. The revelation to the modern reader, if not the protagonist himself, is that the dragons are actually misinterpreted dinosaur bones. This was not my creative imagination. It is based on a strongly supported theory by Adrienne Mayor in her book, *The First Fossil Hunters: Dinosaurs, Mammoths, and Myth in Greek and Roman Times.* She argues that modern paleontology with its discovery and categorization of dinosaur bones is

33

a relatively recent discipline of the 18th and 19th centuries. Until that time, most people did not know about the "terrible lizards."

But our ancient ancestors did. They just didn't realize it. Occasionally, explorers or scholars would stumble across dinosaur bones in their explorations or travels, but didn't know what they were. So they called them dragons, griffons, giants and other mythological beings. Mayor examines dozens of examples of classical Greek and Roman writers' descriptions of mythical monsters that fit the pictures of dinosaur remains.

She writes that the Chinese too found dinosaur fossils and called them dragons. "It is generally believed that the earliest written descriptions of "dragon" bones appeared in a Chinese chronicle of the second century B.C. During the digging of a canal in north-central China, "dragon bones were found and therefore the canal was named Dragon-Head Waterway."[16]

There could not be two more opposite pictures than the ancient Eastern and Western symbols of the dragon. But rather than casting Chinese dragon imagery as inherently satanic, it actually reveals a much deeper nuanced picture of a civilization that had once maintained biblical roots, but fell with the introduction of the dragon and its false gods. So let's take a look at that primeval religion of the land of ancient Tianxia (China).

---

[16] Adrienne Mayor, *The First Fossil Hunters: Dinosaurs, Mammoths, and Myth in Greek and Roman Times,* (Princeton University Press), Kindle Edition. (Kindle Locations 1220-1223).

Shang Di

Until the first emperor of Qin, ancient China actually worshipped a single creator God whose name was Shang Di (or Di or Tian). As Dr. Thong explains, "'Shang' means 'above' or 'supreme' and 'Di' means 'Lord,' 'emperor' or 'God.'" So Shang Di would mean "emperor of heaven" or "the sovereign above all rulers."[17] The use of "Di" in the emperor Qin Shi Huang Di's name therefore indicates his claim to divine status.

Shang Di's attributes matched those of the biblical Yahweh. He was considered by the ancient Chinese to be fatherly, sovereign, eternal, immutable, all-powerful, all-knowing, ever-present, infinite, holy, loving, grace-filled, compassionate and just—just like Yahweh of the Old Testament.[18] This may not sound as significant to our western minds that are saturated in the Judeo-Christian understanding of God's attributes. But in the ancient world, those traits stood out from the common notions of a pantheon of capricious deities with limited agency and contentious motivations squabbling for power.

Like Hebrew religion and unlike all other religions, Shang Di was considered to be a father in the eyes of ancient Chinese religion. Also like Hebrew religion and unlike all other religions, visual images of Shang Di were forbidden. There are no pictures of him in Chinese history.[19] This would make the Hebrews and the Chinese the only

---

[17] Dr. Thong, *Faith Of Our Fathers*, Kindle edition, Location 96 of 344.

[18] Dr. Thong, *Faith Of Our Fathers*, Kindle edition, Location 102-118 of 344.

[19] Dr. Thong, *Faith Of Our Fathers*, Kindle edition, Location 100 of 344.

peoples of that time who prohibited images of the Creator. Every other nation was awash in images of their gods.

Lines from a song of the Border Sacrifice (explained below), called "Song of Central Peace," reads like a Chinese translation of Yahweh creating the heavens and earth of Genesis 1.

> Of old in the beginning, there was the great chaos,
>   without form and dark.
> The five planets had not begun to revolve, more the
>   two lights to shine.
> In the midst of it there existed neither form nor sound.
> You, O Spiritual Sovereign, came forth in your
>   sovereignty, and first did separate the impure from
>   the pure.
> You made heaven; You made earth; You made man.
>   All things became alive with reproducing power.[20]

In the sixteenth century, Jesuit priest Matteo Ricci became the first Western advisor to Emperor Wan Li and established mission bases in China that resulted in the conversion of thousands of Chinese to Christ. To this day, he remains one of the rare western foreigners still highly respected in Chinese history because of his love and accurate understanding of the Chinese culture. He wrote in his book, *The True Meaning*, "Having leafed through a great number of ancient books, it is

---

http://allthechildrenoflight.wordpress.com/2013/02/03/the-creator-god-in-ancient-china-genesis-hidden-in-the-chinese-language/

[20] Dr. Thong, *Faith Of Our Fathers*, Kindle edition, Location 286-288 of 344.

quite clear to me that the Sovereign on High [Bible] and Lord of Heaven [China] are different only in name."[21]

Border Sacrifice

The system of worship of Shang Di was also similar to Old Testament worship. Before the Qin empire, the various kings would perform animal sacrifices to Shang Di that they called "border sacrifices," consisting of a burnt sacrifice of a bull, without blemish, by the sovereign on an "altar of heaven."[22] Some of this annual ceremony shows up in the storyline of *Qin: Dragon Emperor of China*. It was originally performed on Mount Tai in coastal Shandong by previous rulers which is why it was called "border sacrifice."[23] The ritual had lasted through the entire previous eighteen dynasties of China's history, going back 4000 years.[24]

Dr. Thong describes the details of the ceremony from ancient sources to show its similarity to the biblical ceremony engaged in by the Levitical priests of Old Testament Israel. The notion of blood covenant, of substitutionary sacrifice of an animal without blemish reflects the Old Testament sacrificial imagery of Messiah, ultimately fulfilled in the New Covenant of Jesus Christ.[25]

---

[21] http://allthechildrenoflight.wordpress.com/2013/02/03/the-creator-god-in-ancient-china-genesis-hidden-in-the-chinese-language/

[22] John Ross, *The Original Religion of China*, (New York, NY: Eaton and Mains, 1909), 50.

[23] Dr. Thong, *Faith Of Our Fathers*, Kindle edition, Location 128 of 344.

[24] James Legge, *The Chinese Classics* (Vol. III), pp 33–34, The Shoo King: Canon of Shun, Taipei, Southern Materials Centre Inc., 1983.

[25] Dr. Thong, *Faith Of Our Fathers*, Kindle edition, Location 130-162 of 344.

The Altar of Heaven was not a temple, because Shang Di does not dwell in temples built with hands. It was an altar, and it would be built wherever the capital city was for the ruler. The famous Temple of Heaven (more accurately, "Altar of Heaven") in modern day Beijing is an imperial altar first built during the reign of Cheng Zhong (1295-1307) and rebuilt during the Ming dynasty of 1402-1424. It is the largest altar in the world for the worship of God as the ancient Chinese understood him. There are no idols or statues inside it.

But that's not all. The Chinese understanding of Shang Di was also quite similar to the Deuteronomy 32 worldview or Watcher paradigm of Psalm 82 that was explained earlier from the Bible.

Let's take a closer look at that paradigm.

The Lesser Deities

In the Nineteenth Century, Missionary John Ross wrote about the original religion of China as being quite similar to the biblical picture of a divine council of heavenly host called "gods" (*elohim*), that surrounds Yahweh's heavenly throne and do his bidding (Psalm 82). The ancient Chinese spiritual worldview also contained a divine council whose spiritual host were called "shen." Ross explains the primeval Chinese picture thus:

> There is one Supreme Being over all in heaven and on earth, the Ruler alike of gods and men. The inferior deities exist, not as the rivals of God but as faithful ministers of His. God has deputed to each of the inferior deities his own particular sphere of influence

38

and of work. In his own sphere this deity exercises supreme jurisdiction over man, but under God... the references to the "host" of inferior deities clearly indicate not only that these deities were inferior, but that they were entirely subordinate. Yet they were superior to man, whom, in carrying out the will of God, they could protect, reward, or punish, according to his deeds.[26]

Compare this to Psalm 82, and 1 Kings 22 and the similarities are startlingly obvious.

> Psalm 82:1–4
> God has taken his place in the divine council;
>> in the midst of the gods he holds judgment:
> "How long will you judge unjustly
>> and show partiality to the wicked? *Selah*
> Give justice to the weak and the fatherless;
>> maintain the right of the afflicted and the destitute.
> Rescue the weak and the needy;
>> deliver them from the hand of the wicked."

A re-reading of Ross' description of the Chinese divine council above illustrates that it could be applied in its entirety to the divine council of Psalm 82. A supreme creator with inferior "gods" as faithful subordinate ministers carrying out his will in specific spheres or territories.

---

[26] Ross, *The Original Religion of China,* 144-145.

William Boone, another missionary of the nineteenth century, made it even more clear that a prayer at the Border Sacrifice contained the divine council understanding of the Bible:

> There is a special point, however, in the prayer, to which I wish to call attention—the distinction made between Shang-Te, and all the *shin*, or, as I translate the word, *spirits*. They are His guards or attendants. Just as Jehovah came from Paran with holy myriads, (Deut 32:2)—as He revealed Himself on Sinai among thousands of angels, (Ps. 68:17) —so do the Chinese believe that when Shang-Te descends to receive their worship offered by the Emperor, He comes attended by ten thousands of spirits. He is not one of them, though He is "a spirit."[27]

And these *shen* or spirits were also called "bright ones," much like the "shining ones" of Yahweh's heavenly host.[28] Divine beings are often described as shining with brilliance and glory in both the Old Testament (Ex 34:29; Ezek 1:4–7, 27–28; Dan 10:6) as well as the New Testament (Matt 28:3; Luke 24:4).

What could account for this amazing similarity without precedent? Some researchers argue that the Chinese had migrated from Babel and were cut off from other nations, maintaining a less corrupt understanding of their Creator than the other Gentile nations that had devolved into idol worship.[29]

---

[27] James Legge, DD, *The Notions of the Chinese Concerning God and Spirits With and Examination of the Defense of an Essay, The Proper Rendering of the Words Elohim and Theos into the Chinese Language by William J. Boone* (Hong Kong: The London Missionary Society, 1852), 24-25.

[28] Ross, *The Original Religion of China*, 172.

[29] Ross, *The Original Religion of China*, 144-145.

But the Zhou dynasty of 1100 B.C. changed all that. Shang Di became removed, distant with the declaration of Prince Wu, "Heaven is the universal Father, and Earth the universal Mother." It was a switch from an "intelligent, active, personal, moral and all-powerful Agent" to a materialistic dualism of "heaven and earth."[30]

Taoism, Confucism and Buddhism developed out of this change and by the third century B.C., Emperor Qin rejected the worship of Shang Di outright, and outlawed the ancient religion of the supreme Creator. The altars of heaven were abandoned, as depicted in the novel, and he instituted sacrifices to the pantheon of lesser deities along with his idolatrous despotism.[31]

The Sovereign emperor was supposed to rule as vice regent to God, the highest authority on earth called "the Son of Heaven." He was to carry out the "Mandate of Heaven," that is, Shang Di's decrees of justice. But now, the emperor had become a god.[32]

The Dragon had bitten the heel of Shang Di in China.

At least until Messiah came to crush his head.

---

[30] Ross, *The Original Religion of China*, 63-64, 71.

[31] http://allthechildrenoflight.wordpress.com/2013/02/03/the-creator-god-in-ancient-china-genesis-hidden-in-the-chinese-language/

James Legge, DD, *The Notions of the Chinese Concerning God and Spirits With and Examination of the Defense of an Essay, The Proper Rendering of the Words Elohim and Theos into the Chinese Language by William J. Boone* (Hong Kong: The London Missionary Society, 1852), 55.

Dr. Thong, *Faith Of Our Fathers*, Kindle Edition location 130 of 344.

[32] Ross, *The Original Religion of China*, 128.

Chapter 4:
The Gospel in Chinese

Words as Pictures

Chinese is one of the oldest known languages dating back to at least 2700 B.C. Like other ancient languages, its written form was originally pictographic rather than alphabetic. That means the words were like little pictures of what was being written about. But unlike other languages, Chinese retains some of its graphic history even today.

Here is an example of modern Chinese words along with their ancient precursors that researcher Dr. Thong, Chan Kei has used to illustrate the graphic nature of the language. Notice how the modern version on the left still maintains an iconic element of their origin on the right.[1]

Sheep   Turtle   Fish

---

[1] Dr. Thong, *Faith Of Our Fathers*, Kindle Edition location 64 of 344.

Though the language has evolved through the millennia, and has become more symbolic, Chinese characters still carry embedded within them the stories and meanings of their original pictures.

As Dr Thong explains, pictographs are combined to create ideographs or ideograms, which are still graphic, but a bit more abstract or conceptual. Thus, a picture of a mouth over a tree would mean "wooden mouth" which is a colloquialism that refers to someone who is slow-witted or struck speechless. A single tree is a tree. Two trees would denote a group such as a grove. And three trees in a pictograph would represent a large gathering of trees such as a forest.[2]

Dr. Thong then chronicles many examples of words and phrases that he argues are reflections of biblical influence on the Chinese language. That is, they show concepts that are unique to the biblical worldview that seem to indicate a common origin. I recommend buying his book to learn the fascinating depth of this spiritual connection between China and the Bible. The book is Faith of Our Fathers: Finding God in Ancient China.

Another book from which I drew writing examples of this exchange of biblical ideas was The Discovery of Genesis by C.H. Kang. In my novel, all my examples of explanation of Chinese ideograms are real, drawn from this book. I use some of the following examples that reflect the ancient stories of Genesis:

---

[2] Dr. Thong, *Faith Of Our Fathers*, Kindle Edition location 66 of 344.

"Tempter"

Kang breaks out the various visual elements of the word for "tempter" to show the story from the Garden of Eden. I have reproduced my own image of his breakdown here:

山 + 几 + 田 + 丿 = 鬼 + 林 + 广 = 魔
secret   man   garden   [alive]   devil   trees   cover   tempter

Kang explains, "the devil is placed under the cover of protecting trees. The devil waited for Eve in the forbidden tree, which was located in the middle of the garden next to the tree of life—hence the two trees. Furthermore, he was under cover, being hidden in the tree and also camouflaged as a serpent."[3]

The Chinese word for boat tells the story of Noah's ark.

"Boat"

---

[3] C.H. Kang, *The Discovery of Genesis: how the Truths of Genesis Were Found Hidden in the Chinese Language* (St. Louis, MO: Concordia House, 1979), 4.

舟 + 八 + 口 = 船
vessel　eight　mouths　　boat

Kang explains the ideogram for "boat": "There are three elements pictured: a vessel, eight, and mouth, meaning "people." The word for boat, then, tells the story of this first great ark which, in spite of the years of warning and pleading by Noah to his compatriots, had just eight passengers."[4]

The story of the Tower of Babel from the Bible also finds its way into the Chinese word for "tower."

"Tower"

人 + 一 + 口 = 合 + 艹 = 荅 + 土 = 塔
mankind　one　mouth　united　grass　undertake　clay　tower
　　　　　　[speech]　　　　　　　　　[brick]

Kang explains the Babel story embedded in the word,

> On the left side of the figure, artistically accommodating itself to the slope of the tower is the radical dirt, clay, of which the bricks were made. They had boasted, "'Come, let us make bricks, and burn them thoroughly.' And they had brick for stone, and bitumen for mortar" (Genesis 11:3). Then they united, joined together in their rebellion against God. The

4 Kang, *The Discovery of Genesis*, 95.

Chinese placed upon the pinnacle of the tower the sign of Adam's curse , recognizing the folly of this venture. (It would be unlikely that weeds would grow on top of a brick tower!) One other aspect of the character might also have importance. They were originally all of one speech: [men]; [one]; [speech]. Adding the grass on the top, means to undertake. The Chinese themselves built no towers or pagodas until the Buddhist era. This character for tower must surely, therefore, refer to the Tower of Babel.[5]

Because of the technical nature of the linguistics involved, I will refrain from any more examples, lest I become guilty of plagiarism for copying too many large portions of Kang's text. I recommend getting the book to explore the issue more in depth: The Discovery of Genesis: how the Truths of Genesis Were Found Hidden in the Chinese Language by C.H. Kang.

Conclusion

I hope this booklet of research notes was enlightening for those who have read the novel *Qin: Dragon Emperor of China*. It is not exhaustive and is more a compendium of notes for the background of the novel than an attempt to make a sustained argument for the issues brought up in the text. If you want more, please check the footnotes for books and online articles that go into further detail.

---

[5] Kang, *The Discovery of Genesis,* 106.

If you have not read the novel *Qin* yet, you can get it here at Amazon (paid link) in ebook, paperback or audiobook.

• • • • •

If you liked this book, then please help me out by writing a positive review of it on Amazon here. That is one of the best ways to say thank you to me as an author. It really does help my sales and status. Thanks!
– *Brian Godawa*

More Books by Brian Godawa
See www.Godawa.com for more information on other books by Brian Godawa. Check out his other series below:

Chronicles of the Nephilim
Chronicles of the Nephilim is a saga that charts the rise and fall of the Nephilim giants of Genesis 6 and their place in the evil plans of the fallen angelic Sons of God called, "The Watchers." The story starts in the days of Enoch and continues on through the Bible until the arrival of the Messiah, Jesus. The prelude to Chronicles of the Apocalypse. ChroniclesOfTheNephilim.com. (paid link)

Chronicles of the Apocalypse
Chronicles of the Apocalypse is an origin story of the most controversial book of the Bible: Revelation. An historical conspiracy thriller quadrilogy in first century Rome set against the backdrop of explosive spiritual warfare of Satan and his demonic Watchers. ChroniclesOfTheApocalypse.com. (paid link)

Chronicles of the Watchers
Chronicles of the Watchers is a series that charts the influence of spiritual principalities and powers over the course of human history. The kingdoms of man in service to the gods of the nations at war. Completely based on ancient historical and mythological research. ChroniclesOfTheWatchers.com. (paid link)

Great Offers By Brian Godawa

Get the Novel Qin, That is Based on the Biblical Research of This Booklet You are Reading.

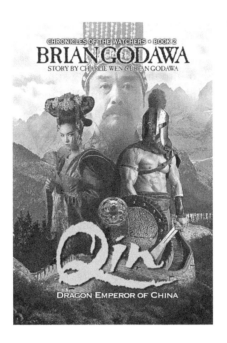

2 Epic Storytellers. A Clash of Ancient Civilizations.

A novel of the first Chinese emperor, the Great Wall of China, spiritual warfare, dragons, and the tower of Babel from the Bible.

https://godawa.com/get-qin/

Brian Godawa

About the Author

Brian Godawa is the screenwriter for the award-winning feature film, *To End All Wars*, starring Kiefer Sutherland. It was awarded the Commander in Chief Medal of Service, Honor and Pride by the Veterans of Foreign Wars, won the first Heartland Film Festival by storm, and showcased the Cannes Film Festival Cinema for Peace.

He previously adapted to film the best-selling supernatural thriller novel *The Visitation* by author Frank Peretti for Ralph Winter (*X-Men, Wolverine*), and wrote and directed *Wall of Separation*, a PBS documentary, and *Lines That Divide*, a documentary on stem cell research.

Mr. Godawa's scripts have won multiple awards in respected screenplay competitions, and his articles on movies and philosophy have been published around the world. He has traveled around the United States teaching on movies, worldviews, and culture to colleges, churches and community groups.

His popular book *Hollywood Worldviews: Watching Films with Wisdom and Discernment* (InterVarsity Press) is used as a textbook in schools around the country. In the Top 10 of Biblical Fiction on Amazon, his first novel series, *Chronicles of the Nephilim*, is an imaginative retelling of Biblical stories of the Nephilim giants, the secret plan of the fallen Watchers, and the War of the Seed of the Serpent with the Seed of Eve. The sequel series, *Chronicles of the Apocalypse*, tells the story of the apostle John's book of Revelation, and *Chronicles of the Watchers* recounts true history through the Watcher paradigm.

Find out more about his other books, lecture tapes and DVDs for sale at his website, www.godawa.com.

Brian Godawa

Brian Godawa

Made in the USA
Las Vegas, NV
14 August 2023

76086349R00036